Cloze Encounters

Grades 5-6

Written by
Rik McGuinness

Published by
World Teachers Press®

Published with the permission of R.I.C. Publications Pty. Ltd.

Copyright © 2000 by Didax, Inc., Rowley, MA 01969. All rights reserved.

First published by R.I.C. Publications Pty. Ltd., Perth, Western Australia.

Printed in the United States of America.

Order Number 2-5122
ISBN 1-58324-046-2

A B C D E F 03 02 01 00

Educational Resources
395 Main Street
Rowley, MA 01969
www.worldteacherspress.com

Foreword

This book is the third of three in the *Cloze Encounters* series. In this book, based on *Space*, each topic is covered on three pages. The first page contains a passage and leading questions to encourage students to take notes. The second page is a cloze passage of the previous page with every tenth word deleted. The third page is a comprehension page which covers the three levels of questioning and some basic word study of topic words.

This book of blackline masters can be used in many ways and with any ability group. It is designed to be flexible in its use.

Answers for the cloze and comprehension pages have been included to save you correcting time.

Contents

Teachers Notes

Each topic contains three pages: a comprehension passage, a cloze page and a comprehension page. You may use all three together or mix and match. For example, you may use the passage and the comprehension page only. This allows for flexibility within the book to suit your individual program.

The Milky Way

Our entire Solar System is just a tiny part of the galaxy called the Milky Way. Galaxies are large groups of stars, dust, gases and planets clustered together. Our Milky Way is just one of many galaxies existing within the universe. The Milky Way contains hundreds of billions of stars and is shaped like a thin disk with a bulge in the center. From this central bulge are curved arms of stars, planets and dust forming a spiral shape. The Milky Way is known as a spiral galaxy. Our Solar System sits on the outer edge of one of those spiral arms.

All stars in the Milky Way orbit its center just like the planets in our Solar System orbit the Sun. Our Sun completes one orbit of the galaxy every 250 million years. The central bulge of the galaxy has a vast number of older stars. Both the bulge and disk are surrounded by a sphere of stars known as a "halo." Scientists believe that within the center of that bulge is a large black hole. Black holes are invisible objects whose gravitational pull is so great that everything gets sucked into them, including the light.

Scientists measure distances between stars and galaxies in "light years." A light year is the distance light travels in one year. Our galaxy is one hundred thousand light years across. Light travels at nearly 300,000 kilometers per second, so these distances are very large.

Write key notes below about the Milky Way. Use these questions to help you with your note taking.

1. What is a galaxy?   2. What does our galaxy look like?
3. How big is our galaxy?

Comprehension Passage

The passage has been written specifically to suit students in grades 5–6. The information given is high-interest to keep the students' attention and contains interesting facts that students love.

Note taking

This feature is a form of comprehension to reiterate what they have learned immediately after reading the text. This helps students clarify what they have just read.

Cloze

This procedure, where systematic deletions have been made, can be used as a teaching technique. If used in conjunction with the previous page, students are required to write appropriate words based on prior knowledge and understanding of the text.

If it is used on its own, it can be used to test students' ability to make appropriate predictions.

Students' answers should indicate some of the following:

• understanding context;
• developing meaning of storyline throughout the passage; and
• displaying a knowledge of the patterns of language.

The Milky Way

Our entire Solar System is just a tiny part

_____ [1] the galaxy called the Milky

Way. Galaxies are large _____ [2] of stars, dust, gases and planets clustered

together. Our _____ [3] Way is just one of many galaxies existing within

_____ [4] universe. The Milky Way contains hundreds of billions of

_____ [5] and is shaped like a thin disk with a _____ [6] in the center.

From this central bulge are curved _____ [7] of stars, planets and dust forming a

spiral shape. _____ [8] Milky Way is known as a spiral galaxy. Our

_____ [9] System sits on the outer edge of one of _____ [10] spiral arms.

All stars in the Milky Way orbit _____ [11] center just like the planets in our Solar

System _____ [12] the Sun. Our Sun completes one orbit of the _____ [13]

every 250 million years. The central bulge of the _____ [14] has a vast number of

older stars. Both the _____ [15] and disk are surrounded by a sphere of stars

_____ [16] as a "halo." Scientists believe that within the center _____ [17]

that bulge is a large black hole. Black holes _____ [18] invisible objects whose

gravitational pull is so great that _____ [19] gets sucked into them, including the

light.

Scientists measure _____ [20] between stars and galaxies in "light years." A light

_____ [21] is the distance light travels in one year. Our _____ [22] is

100,000 light years across. Light travels at nearly _____ [23] kilometers per second,

so these distances are very large.

Teachers Notes

The Milky Way

1. What are galaxies?

_____

_____

_____

2. What type of galaxy is the Milky Way?

_____

_____

3. Describe this type of galaxy.

_____

_____

4. How are the Milky Way and our Solar System alike? _____

_____

5. What is a light year? _____

6. If you could travel at the speed of light, how long would it take you to travel across the Milky Way?

_____

7. (i) What do scientists believe is at the centre of the Milky Way?

_____

_____

  (ii) What effect can this have?_____

8. What is a 'halo' and where can it be found? _____

_____

_____

9. You are an astronaut whose spacecraft has just reached the edge of a giant black hole. You have collected important scientific data to return to base. On leaving, however, something goes wrong and instead of moving away from the black hole you are being drawn by its gravitational pull into the hole. Where does your journey take you? What happens along the way? Write a story about your adventure.

Comprehension

The three levels of questioning have been covered on every comprehension page, ensuring students gain practice at the literal, inferential and evaluative levels (L, I, E).

The Milky Way

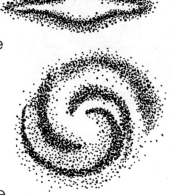

Our entire Solar System is just a tiny part of the galaxy called the Milky Way. Galaxies are large groups of stars, dust, gases and planets clustered together. Our Milky Way is just one of many galaxies existing within the universe. The Milky Way contains hundreds of billions of stars and is shaped like a thin disk with a bulge in the center. From this central bulge are curved arms of stars, planets and dust forming a spiral shape. The Milky Way is known as a spiral galaxy. Our Solar System sits on the outer edge of one of those spiral arms.

All stars in the Milky Way orbit its center just like the planets in our Solar System orbit the Sun. Our Sun completes one orbit of the galaxy every 250 million years. The central bulge of the galaxy has a vast number of older stars. Both the bulge and disk are surrounded by a sphere of stars known as a "halo." Scientists believe that within the center of that bulge is a large black hole. Black holes are invisible objects whose gravitational pull is so great that everything gets sucked into them, including light.

Scientists measure distances between stars and galaxies in "light years." A light year is the distance light travels in one year. Our galaxy is one hundred thousand light years across. Light travels at nearly 300,000 kilometers per second, so these distances are extremely large.

Write key notes below about the Milky Way. Use these questions to help you with your note taking.

1. What is a galaxy?
2. What does our galaxy look like?
3. How big is our galaxy?

- _____
- _____
- _____
- _____
- _____
- _____
- _____

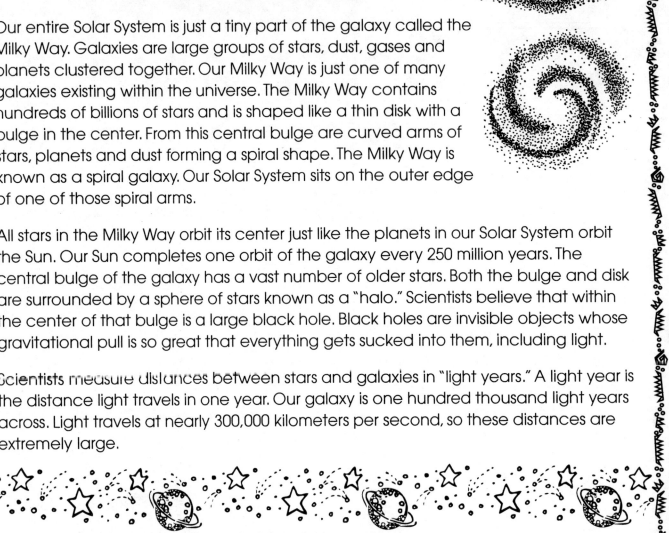

The Milky Way

Our entire Solar System is just a tiny part

_____1 the galaxy called the Milky

Way. Galaxies are large _____2 of stars, dust, gases and planets clustered

together. Our _____3 Way is just one of many galaxies existing within

_____4 universe. The Milky Way contains hundreds of billions of

_____5 and is shaped like a thin disk with a _____6 in the center.

From this central bulge are curved _____7 of stars, planets and dust forming a

spiral shape. _____8 Milky Way is known as a spiral galaxy. Our

_____9 System sits on the outer edge of one of _____10 spiral arms.

All stars in the Milky Way orbit _____11 center just like the planets in our Solar

System _____12 the Sun. Our Sun completes one orbit of the _____13

every 250 million years. The central bulge of the _____14 has a vast number of

older stars. Both the _____15 and disk are surrounded by a sphere of stars

_____16 as a "halo." Scientists believe that within the center _____17

that bulge is a large black hole. Black holes _____18 invisible objects whose

gravitational pull is so great that _____19 gets sucked into them, including light.

Scientists measure _____20 between stars and galaxies in "light years." A light

_____21 is the distance light travels in one year. Our _____22 is

100,000 light years across. Light travels at nearly _____23 kilometers per second,

so these distances are extremely large.

The Milky Way

1. What are galaxies?

_____

_____

_____

_____

2. What type of galaxy is the Milky Way?

_____

_____

_____

3. Describe this type of galaxy.

_____

_____

4. How are the Milky Way and our Solar System alike? _____

_____

_____

5. What is a light year? _____

_____

6. If you could travel at the speed of light, how long would it take you to travel across the Milky Way?

_____

7.(a) What do scientists believe is at the center of the Milky Way?

_____

_____

(b) What effect can this have?_____

_____

8. What is a "halo" and where can it be found? _____

_____

9. You are an astronaut whose spacecraft has just reached the edge of a giant black hole. You have collected important scientific data to return to base. On leaving, however, something goes wrong and instead of moving away from the black hole you are being drawn by its gravitational pull into the hole. Where does your journey take you? What happens along the way? Write a story about your adventure.

The Solar System

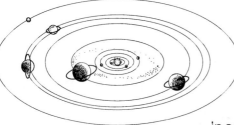

Our Solar System exists within a vast universe. It is part of the galaxy called the Milky Way. The Solar System is shaped like a disk. It consists of a star called the Sun and all the objects that travel around it. These objects include nine planets and their moons, meteoroids, asteroids, comets and dust.

The Sun is the center of our Solar System. It is about 600 times bigger than all the objects in the Solar System put together. Each planet varies in size and distance from the Sun. The orbits of the planets do not cross, with the exception of Pluto, whose path crosses over the orbital path of Neptune. The order of the planets from the closest to the furthest away from the Sun is Mercury, Venus, Earth, Mars, Jupiter, Saturn, Uranus, Neptune and Pluto.

Thousands of minor planets, called asteroids, also orbit the Sun. These small objects are made from metal or rock. Many of them are found circling the Sun in a broad "asteroid belt" between the orbits of Mars and Jupiter. Asteroids can also be known as planetoids. Meteoroids are left-over pieces of rock, metal, or gas after the collision of asteroids or the breaking up of a comet. Comets are small bodies made of frozen gases with a long tail of dust and gases that escape from the head, or nucleus.

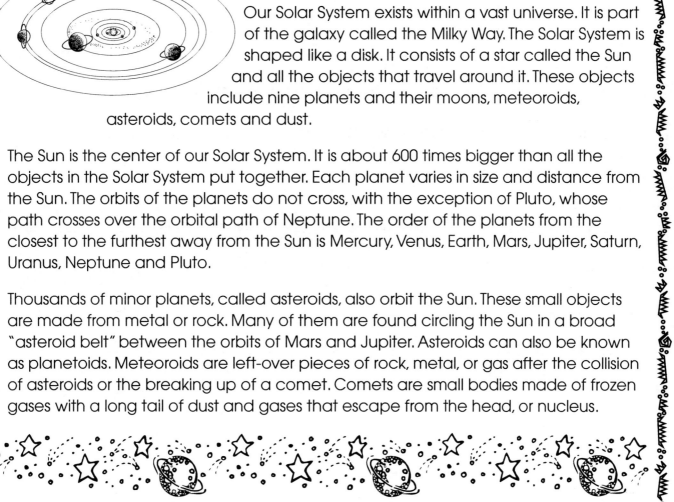

Write key notes below about the Solar System. Use these questions to help you with your note taking.

1. What is the Solar System?
2. What is a comet?
3. What is the order of the planets in our Solar System?
4. What is the difference between asteroids and meteoroids?

- _____
- _____
- _____
- _____
- _____
- _____
- _____

The Solar System

Our Solar System exists within a vast universe. It _____[1] part of the galaxy

called the Milky Way. The _____[2] System is shaped like a disk. It consists of

_____[3] star called the Sun and all the objects that _____[4]

around it. These objects include nine planets and their _____[5], meteoroids,

asteroids, comets and dust.

The Sun is the _____[6] of our Solar System. It is about 600 _____[7]

bigger than all the objects in the Solar System _____[8] together. Each

planet varies in size and distance from _____[9] Sun. The orbits of the planets

do not cross, with the exception of Pluto, whose path crosses _____[10] the

orbital path of Neptune. The order of the _____[11] from the closest to the

furthest away from the _____[12] is Mercury, Venus, Earth, Mars, Jupiter,

Saturn, Uranus, Neptune _____[13] Pluto.

Thousands of minor planets, called asteroids, also orbit _____[14] Sun. These

small objects are made from metal or _____[15]. Many of them are found

circling the Sun in _____[16] broad "asteroid belt" between the orbits of Mars

and _____[17]. Asteroids can also be known as planetoids. Meteoroids are

_____[18] pieces of rock, metal or gas after the collision _____[19]

asteroids or the breaking up of a comet. Comets _____[20] small

bodies made of frozen gases with a long _____[21] of dust

and gases that escape from the head,

_____[22] nucleus.

The Solar System

1. What does our Solar System consist of?

_____

_____

_____

2. Name our galaxy.

_____

3. Give two reasons why our Sun is important to our Solar System.

(a) _____

_____

(b) _____

_____

4. Describe an asteroid. _____

_____

5. Circle the correct answer.
   Meteoroids are…

   (a) small rock objects orbiting in a "belt" around the Sun.

   (b) frozen gases.

   (c) left-over metal or rock pieces resulting from the collision of asteroids or the break-up of a comet.

6. Explain the orbital path of Pluto. _____

_____

_____

7. Name these space objects.

   (a) the planet furthest from the Sun _____

   (b) the planet closest to the Sun _____

   (c) a frozen gas ball with a tail _____

   (d) a minor planet _____

   (e) another name for an asteroid _____

8. What do you think would happen if the planets didn't travel in orbits around the Sun?

_____

_____

9. How many words can you make from the letters in **Solar System**?

The Sun

The Sun is by far the largest object in our Solar System. It is an enormous ball of hot, glowing gas which is the center of our Solar System. All the planets travel around it at different speeds. It appears to be big and bright, however, it is not the largest star in the galaxy. The Sun is 150 million kilometers away from Earth. Light from the Sun takes eight minutes to reach us, whereas light from the next nearest star, Sirius, takes eight years! Scientists call our Sun a "yellow dwarf." Some stars are over 1,000 times larger than our Sun and are called "supergiants."

The Sun is made up of gases, mostly hydrogen and some helium. At the center, or core, the Sun's temperature is around fifteen million degrees Celsius. Scientists think that the Sun has shone in the sky for nearly five billion years and believe it has enough hydrogen fuel to "burn" for another five to six billion years.

This giant star gives our Earth essential light and heat needed for survival on our planet. Without the Sun there would be no life on Earth. Plants use the Sun's light when making their food. When a plant does this, it gives off oxygen. Animals eat the plants and breathe the oxygen. The animals then breathe out carbon dioxide which the plants combine with the Sun's light and water to make more food, continuing the cycle of life on our planet.

Write key notes below about the Sun. Use these questions to help you with your note taking.

1. Why is the Sun important in our Solar System?

2. What is the Sun made of?   3. Why is the Sun so important to us on Earth?

- _____

- _____

- _____

- _____

- _____

- _____

- _____

The Sun

The Sun is by far the largest object in _____¹ Solar System. It is an enormous

ball of hot, _____² gas which is the center of our Solar System.

_____³ the planets travel around it at different speeds. It _____⁴

to be big and bright, however, it is not _____⁵ largest star in the galaxy. The

Sun is 150 _____⁶ kilometers away from Earth. Light from the Sun takes

_____⁷ minutes to reach us, whereas light from the next _____⁸

star, Sirius, takes eight years! Scientists call our Sun _____⁹ "yellow dwarf."

Some stars are over 1,000 times larger _____¹⁰ our Sun

and are called "supergiants."

The Sun is _____¹¹ up of gases, mostly

hydrogen and some helium. At _____¹² center, or core, the Sun's

temperature is around fifteen _____¹³ degrees Celsius. Scientists think that

the Sun has shone _____¹⁴ the sky for nearly five billion years and believe

_____¹⁵ has enough hydrogen fuel to "burn" for another five

_____¹⁶ six billion years.

This giant star gives our Earth _____¹⁷ light and heat needed for survival on

our planet. _____¹⁸ the Sun there would be no life on Earth. _____¹⁹

use the Sun's light when making their food. When _____²⁰ plant does this, it

gives off oxygen. Animals eat _____²¹ plants and breathe the oxygen. The

animals then breathe _____²² carbon dioxide which the plants combine

with the Sun's _____²³ and water to make more food, continuing the cycle

_____²⁴ life on our planet.

The Sun

1. *True or false.* Shade the correct answer.

   (a) The Sun is the largest object in our Solar System. | True / False |

   (b) Light takes eight minutes to reach us from the Sun. | True / False |

   (c) The Sun is a planet. | True / False |

   (d) Scientists call our Sun a "supergiant." | True / False |

2. What is the name of our next nearest star? _____

3. Describe a "supergiant."   **4.** List two facts about the surface of the Sun.

   _____   (a)_____

   _____   _____

   _____   (b)_____

   _____   _____

5. Explain how plants, animals and the Sun work together for survival on our planet.

   _____

   _____

   _____

   _____

6. Life on _____ depends on _____ and _____ from the Sun.

7. Shade the words that best describe the Sun.

"supergiant"	largest star in galaxy	hot gases	star
"yellow dwarf"	essential to life on Earth	center of Solar System	mostly helium

8. Imagine the Sun is losing its powerful energy. Write a newspaper headline for such an event.

Mercury

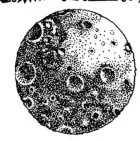

Mercury is the closest planet to the Sun and is less than half the size of the Earth. Due to Mercury's size and closeness to the Sun's bright glare, it is often hard to see from the Earth without a telescope.

Mercury travels around the Sun in an elliptical orbit and moves faster than any other planet. The ancient Romans named the planet after the "swift messenger" of their gods, probably because it traveled so quickly across the sky. It takes only eighty-eight days to travel around the Sun once. The Earth takes just over 365 days to do the same thing. Mercury rotates slowly on its axis, so a day on Mercury is almost as long as sixty Earth days.

The surface of Mercury is very much like that of our Moon. It has steep cliffs, flat plains and many deep craters. Many scientists believe these craters were formed by meteorites and comets hitting its surface. Mercury is very dry and hot and has no real air. The temperature on the planet's surface may reach as high as 420°C, hot enough to melt lead. Since there is a lack of atmosphere, Mercury's sky is black and stars would probably be visible from its surface by day. On the dark side, facing away from the Sun, or at night, temperatures can drop to –173°C, colder than the Earth's South Pole. None of the plant or animal life on Earth could survive on Mercury due to the intense temperatures and the lack of oxygen.

Write key notes about Mercury. Use these questions to help you with your note taking.

1. Where is Mercury located?   2. How did it get its name?

3. What is the surface of Mercury like?

- _____

- _____

- _____

- _____

- _____

- _____

- _____

- _____

Mercury

Mercury is the closest planet to the Sun and _____[1] less than

half the size of the Earth. Due _____[2] Mercury's size

and closeness to the Sun's bright glare, _____[3] is often

hard to see from the Earth without _____[4] telescope.

Mercury travels around the Sun in an elliptical _____[5] and

moves faster than any other planet. The ancient _____[6] named the planet

after the "swift messenger" of their _____[7], probably because it traveled

so quickly across the sky. _____[8] takes only eighty-eight days to travel

around the Sun _____[9]. The Earth takes just over 365 days to do

_____[10] same thing. Mercury rotates slowly on its axis, so

_____[11] day on Mercury is almost as long as sixty _____[12] days.

The surface of Mercury is very much like _____[13] of our Moon. It has steep

cliffs, flat plains _____[14] many deep craters. Many scientists believe these

craters were _____[15] by meteorites and comets hitting its surface.

Mercury is _____[16] dry and hot and has no real air. The temperature

_____[17] the planet's surface may reach as high as 420°C,

_____[18] enough to melt lead. Since there is a lack _____[19]

atmosphere, Mercury's sky is black and stars would probably _____[20]

visible from its surface by day. On the dark _____[21], facing away from the

Sun, or at night, temperatures _____[22] drop to −173°C, colder than the

Earth's South Pole. _____[23] of the plant or animal life on Earth could

_____[24] on Mercury due to the intense temperatures and the

_____[25] of oxygen.

Mercury

1. Mercury is the *furthest/closest* planet *from/to* the Sun and is about *half the size/twice the size* of the Earth.

2. Why is Mercury often hard to see? _____

_____

3. How long does it take Mercury to travel around the Sun?

_____

4. Explain how Mercury got its name. _____

_____

_____

5. Give three facts about the surface of Mercury.

(a) _____

_____

(b) _____

_____

(c) _____

_____

6. How do scientists believe the craters were formed?

_____

_____

_____

_____

_____

_____

7. Why wouldn't life, like ours on Earth, survive on Mercury? _____

_____

_____

8. What special characteristics do you think an animal would need to be able to live on Mercury?

_____

_____

_____

_____

_____

Draw your animal.

The Moon

The Moon is the Earth's closest neighbor in space. Although the Moon is the brightest object in the night sky, it does not give off its own light. The "moonlight" is only a reflection of light from the Sun. If the Earth was the size of a golf ball, the Moon would be the size of a marble. As the Moon is a lot smaller than the Earth, its gravity is also a lot less. A person who weighs 60 kg on Earth would weigh only 10 kg on the Moon.

Even though the Moon and Earth are very close to each other in space, they are very different from each other. The Earth is a blue, watery, cloud-covered planet, filled with living things. The Moon is a barren place with no water, air, clouds, or living things. The Moon's surface is covered by thousands of bowl-shaped craters, thought to be formed by meteorites or asteroids crashing into it. The surface is also covered with mountains, hills, valleys and flat plains. The temperature can vary between –240°C and 130°C.

More is known about our Moon than any other object in space, as it is the only object in space to be visited by humans. In 1969, Neil Armstrong became the first person to set foot on the Moon. He was one of three astronauts aboard the spacecraft Apollo 11 that landed on the Moon on July 20, 1969. Other successful expeditions followed, providing a means of studying the Moon in more accurate detail.

Write key notes about the Moon. Use these questions to help you with your note taking.

1. Why does the Moon "shine"?   2. What is the Moon's surface like?

3. Why do we know so much about the Moon?

- _____
- _____
- _____
- _____
- _____
- _____
- _____
- _____
- _____

The Moon

The Moon is the Earth's closest neighbor in space. _____[1] the Moon is the

brightest object in the night _____[2], it does not give off its own light. The

"_____"[3] is only a reflection of light from the Sun. _____[4] the

Earth was the size of a golf ball, _____[5] Moon would be the size of a marble.

As _____[6] Moon is a lot smaller than the Earth, its

_____[7] is also a lot less. A person who weighs

_____[8] on Earth would weigh only 10 kg on the Moon.

_____[9] though the Moon and Earth are very close to

_____[10] other in space, they are very different from each

_____[11]. The Earth is a blue, watery, cloud-covered

planet, filled _____[12] living things. The Moon is a barren

place with _____[13] water, air, clouds, or living things. The Moon's surface

_____[14] covered by thousands of bowl-shaped craters, thought to be

_____[15] by meteorites or asteroids crashing into it. The _____[16] is

also covered with mountains, hills, valleys and flat _____[17]. The temperature

can vary between –240°C and 130°C.

More _____[18] known about our Moon than any other object in

_____[19], as it is the only object in space to _____[20] visited by

humans. In 1969, Neil Armstrong became the _____[21] person to set foot on

the Moon. He was _____[22] of three astronauts aboard the spacecraft Apollo

11 that _____[23] on the Moon on July 20, 1969. Other successful

_____[24] followed, providing a means of studying the Moon in

_____[25] accurate detail.

The Moon

1. What is "moonlight"? _____

    _____

2. If a person weighs 120 kg on the Earth,
   what will they weigh on the Moon?

    _____

3. Why is it thought life does not exist on the Moon?

    _____

    _____

4. Describe the historic events that occurred in 1969. _____

    _____

    _____

5. What do you think people would need to survive on the Moon?
   Give reasons for your answer.

    _____

    _____

    _____

6. Use the box below to list the differences between the Earth and our Moon.

Earth	Moon

7. Find dictionary meanings for these words.

    (a) barren _____

    (b) gravity _____

8. Complete the word chain using Moon or space words.

    lunareflection

Comets

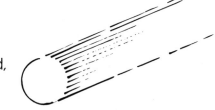

Comets are icy balls that travel through our Solar System, orbiting the Sun. The center of a comet is a hard, icy core called a nucleus. A cloudy atmosphere surrounds the nucleus and is called a coma. Together, the nucleus and coma form the head of a comet. The head of the comet looks a little like a dirty ball of snow. This ball may be less than 16 kilometers in diameter and is made of frozen gases, ice and pieces of rock dust. The gases include ammonia, carbon dioxide, carbon monoxide and methane.

Each time a comet passes close to the Sun, it loses some of its ice and dust. The solar winds blow a stream of gas and dust away from the comet and away from the Sun. This forms the comet's tail. This is a spectacular streak of gas and dust that can trail for millions of kilometers into space.

Some comets eventually lose all their ice and dust. They then become clouds of dust or turn into asteroids. Some pieces of comets can reach the Earth. As they pass through our atmosphere they burn up and are called "meteors" or "shooting stars."

Comets are usually seen only with a telescope, but sometimes, when one is close to the Sun, we can see it without a telescope for several days or even weeks. There are many comets in our Solar System but the best known is Halley's Comet. It was named after Edmund Halley when he successfully predicted its return in 1758 to our skies. He recognized that this comet could be seen on average every seventy-seven years as it orbits the Sun. The comet is now beyond the orbit of Uranus and is expected to return in the year 2062.

Write key notes about comets. Use these questions to help you with your note taking.

1. What are comets?   2. How does the tail of a comet form?

3. Name a famous comet in our Solar System.

- _____
- _____
- _____
- _____
- _____
- _____
- _____

Comets

Comets are icy balls that travel through our Solar _____[1], orbiting the Sun. The center of a comet is _____[2] hard, icy core called a nucleus. A cloudy atmosphere _____[3] the nucleus and is called a coma. Together, the _____[4] and coma form the head of a comet. The _____[5] of the comet looks a little like a dirty _____[6] of snow. This ball may be less than sixteen _____[7] in diameter and is made of frozen gases, ice _____[8] pieces of rock dust. The gases include ammonia, carbon _____[9], carbon monoxide and methane.

Each time a comet passes _____[10] to the Sun, it loses some of its ice _____[11] dust. The solar winds blow a stream of gas _____[12] dust away from the comet and away from the _____[13]. This forms the comet's tail. This is a spectacular _____[14] of gas and dust that can trail for millions _____[15] kilometers into space.

Some comets eventually lose all their _____[16] and dust. They then become clouds of dust or _____[17] into asteroids. Some pieces of comets can reach the _____[18]. As they pass through our atmosphere they burn up _____[19] are called "meteors" or "shooting stars."

Comets are usually _____[20] only with a telescope but sometimes, when one is _____[21] to the Sun, we can see it without a _____[22] for several days or even weeks. There are many _____[23] in our Solar System but the best known is Halley's _____[24]. It was named after Edmund Halley when he successfully _____[25] its return in 1758 to our skies. He recognized _____[26] this comet could be seen on average every seventy-seven _____[27] as it orbits the Sun. The comet is now _____[28] the orbit of Uranus and is expected to return _____[29] the year 2062.

Comets

1. Where can comets be found? _____

2. What is a comet made of? _____

3. Describe these features of a comet.

   (a) nucleus _____

   _____

   (b) tail _____

   _____

   (c) coma _____

   _____

4. What happens when a comet approaches the Sun? _____

_____

_____

5. What is a comet called if it reaches the Earth's atmosphere? _____

_____

6. List three important facts about Halley's Comet.

   (a)_____

   (b)_____

   (c)_____

7. Why do you think comets return after several years of being sighted?

   _____

   _____

   _____

8. Write questions for these answers.

   (a) Edmund Halley _____

   _____

   _____

   (b) "shooting star" _____

   _____

   _____

9. How many words can you find in this spiral?
   Circle them.

cometcstelescoperticemsuidustjsarockknbmeteorsnsocomfvsizemsearthmnoisunmnbspiecesm

Meteors

Meteors are bright streaks of light that can be seen at times in our skies. They are often called "shooting stars" or "falling stars." A meteor can be seen when a piece of metal or rock, called a meteoroid, enters the atmosphere of Earth at a very high speed. Air friction heats the meteoroid so that it is glowing hot and leaves a trail of hot glowing gases. This lasts for only a few seconds. Only a few meteoroids actually reach the surface of the Earth. If they do they are called meteorites. Millions of meteors enter the atmosphere of the Earth every day but very few of them ever become meteorites.

Meteoroids travel in a variety of orbits and speeds around the Sun and enter the Earth's atmosphere at speeds from 11 km/h to 72 km/h.

There are two different types of meteorites—stony and iron. Stony meteorites consist of rock minerals and iron particles combined together. Iron meteorites consist mainly of iron with traces of nickel and other elements. Some may be the size of a marble while others may weigh up to sixty tons. A meteorite must be of substantial size to reach the Earth. If it is too small it will burn up before it reaches the Earth's surface. If it's too big it may explode before reaching the ground.

Scientists collect and study meteorites as they are thought to be made of material unchanged since the time that the planets and moons were formed. Thousands of small meteorites have been found in Antarctica because they have been preserved in the ice.

Write key notes below about meteors. Use these questions to help you with your note taking.

1. What is a meteor?
2. What is a meteorite?
3. From what are meteorites made?
4. Why do scientists find them important?

- _____
- _____
- _____
- _____
- _____
- _____
- _____
- _____

Meteors

Meteors are bright streaks of light that can be _____[1] at times in our skies.

They are often called "_____[2] stars" or "falling stars." A meteor can be seen

_____[3] a piece of metal or rock, called a meteoroid, _____[4] the

atmosphere of Earth at a very high speed. _____[5] friction heats the

meteoroid so that it is glowing _____[6] and leaves a trail of hot glowing

gases. This _____[7] for only a few seconds. Only a few meteoroids

_____[8] reach the surface of the Earth. If they do _____[9] are

called meteorites. Millions of meteors enter the atmosphere _____[10] the

Earth every day but very few of them _____[11] become meteorites.

Meteoroids travel in a variety of orbits _____[12] speeds around the Sun and

enter the Earth's atmosphere _____[13] speeds from 11 km/h to 72 km/h.

There are two different _____[14] of meteorites—stony and iron. Stony

meteorites consist of _____[15] minerals and iron particles combined

together. Iron meteorites consist mainly _____[16] iron with traces of nickel

and other elements. Some _____[17] be the size of a marble while others

may _____[18] up to sixty tons. A meteorite must be of _____[19] size

to reach the Earth. If it is too _____[20] it will burn up before it reaches the

Earth's _____[21]. If it's too big it may explode before reaching

_____[22] ground.

Scientists collect and study meteorites as they are

_____[23] to be made of material unchanged since

the time _____[24] the planets and moons were

formed. Thousands of small _____[25] have been

found in Antarctica because they have been _____ [26] in the ice.

Meteors

1. What is a meteor?

_____

_____

_____

2. Why does a meteor glow?

_____

_____

_____

3. Explain these terms.

(a) meteoroid _____

_____

_____

(b) meteorite _____

_____

4. Why must a meteorite be a substantial size to reach the Earth?

_____

_____

_____

5. Why do you think meteorites are of such interest to scientists?

_____

_____

_____

6. From what can meteorites be made? _____

_____

7. _True or False._ Shade the correct answer.

(a) Meteorites can vary greatly in size. `True / False`

(b) Air friction cools and slows down the meteoroid. `True / False`

(c) Millions of meteors enter the atmosphere everyday. `True / False`

(d) Meteorites can be made from stone or iron. `True / False`

(e) Scientists think meteorites are cooled pieces of the Sun. `True / False`

8. Write a newspaper headline about an out-of-control meteorite falling to Earth.

Asteroids

Most asteroids in our Solar System are found circling the Sun in an orbital belt between Mars and Jupiter. Sometimes called "minor planets," or "planetoids," asteroids are thought to be the small, rocky remains of a planet which broke up millions of years ago, or particles that never came together in the early days of the formation of planets in our Solar System.

Asteroids vary in size and shape. Thousands of the larger asteroids have been named by scientists. Ceres is such an asteroid. The largest and the first to be discovered in 1801, it measures almost 1,000 kilometers in diameter. Pallas, Juno and Vesta are other large asteroids. Most asteroids, however, are much smaller than this, perhaps only six meters in diameter. Some asteroids are made of carbon while others are made of various minerals. All the asteroids combined would not make an object as large as our Moon.

The orbits of asteroids may change slowly due to the gravitational pull of larger planets. Over time these changes may lead to collisions. In 1937, a small asteroid called Hermes came very close to the Earth. Scientists believe that a large asteroid has already collided with our planet. This collision, about sixty-five million years ago, caused major climate and weather changes and probably led to the extinction of the dinosaurs alive at that time.

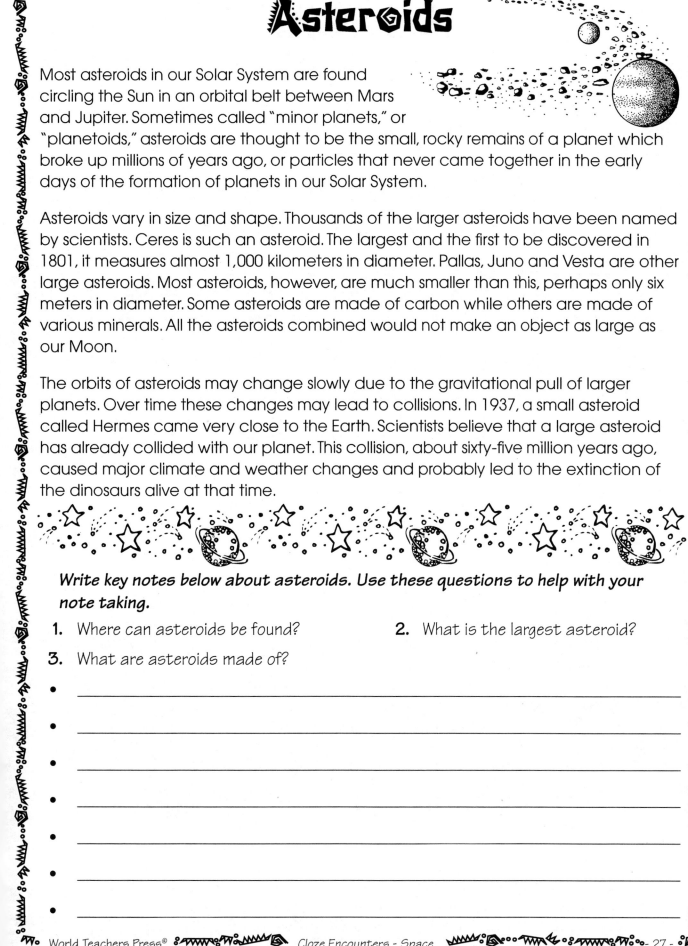

Write key notes below about asteroids. Use these questions to help with your note taking.

1. Where can asteroids be found?
2. What is the largest asteroid?
3. What are asteroids made of?

- _____
- _____
- _____
- _____
- _____
- _____
- _____

Asteroids

Most asteroids in our Solar System are found circling _____[1] Sun in an orbital

belt between Mars and Jupiter. _____[2] called "minor planets," or

"planetoids," asteroids are thought to _____[3] the small, rocky remains of a

planet which broke _____[4] millions of years ago, or particles that never

came _____[5] in the early days of the formation of planets

_____[6] our Solar System.

Asteroids vary in size and shape. _____[7] of the larger asteroids have been

named by scientists. _____[8] is such an asteroid. The largest and the first

_____[9] be discovered in 1801, it measures almost 1,000 kilometers

_____[10] diameter. Pallas, Juno and Vesta are other large asteroids.

_____[11] asteroids, however, are much smaller than this, perhaps only

_____[12] meters in diameter. Some asteroids are made of carbon

_____[13] others are made of various minerals. All the asteroids

_____[14] would not make an object as large as our _____[15].

The orbits of asteroids may change slowly due to _____[16] gravitational pull

of larger planets. Over time these changes _____[17] lead

to collisions. In 1937, a small asteroid called _____[18]

came very close to the Earth. Scientists believe that

_____[19] large asteroid has already collided with our

planet. _____[20] collision, about sixty-five million years ago, caused

_____[21] climate and weather changes and probably led to the

_____[22] of the dinosaurs alive at that time.

Asteroids

1. Where can most asteroids be found? _____

_____

2. How do scientists believe the asteroid belt was formed?

_____

_____

_____

3. Name and describe the largest asteroid.

_____

_____

_____

4. What do scientists believe may have led to the extinction of the dinosaurs?

_____

5. What do you think would happen to life on Earth if it was once again on a collision course with a large asteroid?

_____

_____

6. Find synonyms in the text for these words.

(a) planetoids _____

(b) crash _____

(c) death of a species _____

7. Name a new asteroid just located by scientists.

Name: _____

Description: _____

_____

_____

_____

Reason for name: _____

_____

8. How many words can you find in the spiral? Circle them.

Space

Space continues in all directions, with no known limits, to infinity. It is the area which all objects from the universe move within. All planets, stars and galaxies are minute compared to the vast openness of space.

The Earth is surrounded by air. This air is the atmosphere that protects our planet from space. The further from Earth you go, the thinner the air becomes. The air runs out at about ninety-five kilometers from the Earth's surface. This is where space begins. Outer space, or beyond the atmosphere, is not entirely empty. It contains dust, meteoroids and even thousands of spacecraft that have been launched from Earth.

The space between planets in our Solar System is called "interplanetary space." The Sun's gravity controls the movement of planets in this space to form orbits. Distances in "interplanetary space" are measured in millions of kilometers. For example, the distance between the Earth and the Sun is 150 million kilometers.

The space between the stars is called "interstellar space." The distances in "interstellar space" are measured in light years. This is the distance light travels in one year. The nearest star to the Sun is Proxima Centauri, which is nearly 4.5 light years (45 trillion kilometers) from the Sun.

Beyond this space is "intergalactic space." That is, the space between galaxies, a distance so vast it reaches almost beyond our imaginations!

Write key notes about space. Use these questions to help with your note taking.

1. What is space?   2. When does space start?

3. How are distances measured in space?

- _____
- _____
- _____
- _____
- _____
- _____
- _____

 # Space

Space continues in all directions, with no known limits, _____[1] infinity. It is the

area which all objects _____[2] the universe move within. All planets, stars and

galaxies _____[3] minute compared to the vast openness of space.

The _____[4] is surrounded by air. This air is the atmosphere _____[5]

protects our planet from space. The further from Earth _____[6] go, the thinner

the air becomes. The air runs _____[7] at about ninety-five kilometers from the

Earth's surface. This _____[8] where space begins. Outer space, or beyond the

atmosphere, _____[9] not entirely empty. It contains dust, meteoroids and

even _____[10] of spacecraft that have been launched from Earth.

The _____[11] between planets in our Solar System is called "interplanetary

_____[12]." The Sun's gravity controls the movement of planets in

_____[13] space to form orbits. Distances in "interplanetary space" are

_____[14] in millions of kilometers. For example, the distance between

_____[15] Earth and the Sun is 150 million kilometers.

The _____[16] between the stars is called "interstellar space." The distances

_____[17] "interstellar space" are measured in light years. This is

_____[18] distance light travels in one year. The nearest star _____[19]

the Sun is Proxima Centauri, which is nearly 4.5 _____[20] years (45 trillion

kilometers) from the Sun.

Beyond this _____[21] is "intergalactic space." That is, the space between

galaxies, _____[22] distance so vast it reaches almost beyond our imaginations!

Space

1. What is space? Explain.

_____

_____

_____

2. What protects our planet?

_____

_____

_____

3. How far above the Earth does this air reach? _____

_____

4. List some main facts to explain these "space" terms.

"interplanetary space"	*"interstellar space"*	*"intergalactic space"*

5. What can be found in outer space just beyond our Earth?

_____

_____

6. If you could travel at half the speed of light, how long would it take you to get to Proxima Centauri? _____

7. You have traveled through "intergalactic space" to a planet in another galaxy. Complete the profile on one of the planet's creatures.

Galaxy Name: _____

Planet's Name: _____

Alien's Name: _____

Description: _____

_____

_____

Most Unusual Feature: _____

_____

_____

Photo ID

Spacecraft

People who build spacecraft do so in special factories. These factories need to be very clean as the slightest bit of dust or dirt might later cause major problems.

All parts of the spacecraft are tested many times before being launched into space.

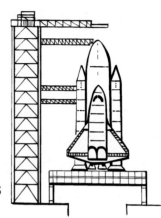

The biggest problem for any spacecraft is getting into space. The Earth's pull, or gravity, is very strong so spacecraft must have rockets fitted to them to help them get into space. To reach space, the rockets need to make the spacecraft attain a speed of eight kilometers per second. This speed is called the "orbital velocity" and happens 190 kilometers above the Earth's surface. The spacecraft can now freely orbit the Earth. However, if the spacecraft is headed for further destinations, such as the Moon, its speed needs to increase to twelve kilometers per second. This speed is called "escape velocity" and means the spacecraft has broken away from the Earth's pull, or gravity.

To travel further again, for example to another planet such as Mars, the spacecraft must be launched from Earth at a velocity (speed and direction) greater than the "escape velocity." The craft would then go into "solar orbit" to carry it to the target planet. The Viking space probe has sent back valuable information from orbiting and landing on Mars.

Write key notes about spacecraft. Use these questions to help you with your note taking.

1. Where are spacecraft made?   2. What is "orbital velocity"?

3. What are rockets used for?

- _____
- _____
- _____
- _____
- _____
- _____
- _____
- _____

Spacecraft

People who build spacecraft do so in special factories. _____[1] factories

need to be very clean as the slightest _____[2] of dust or dirt might later

cause major problems.

_____[3] parts of the spacecraft are tested many times before

_____[4] launched into space.

The biggest problem for any spacecraft _____[5] getting into space. The

Earth's pull, or gravity, is _____[6] strong so spacecraft must have rockets

fitted to them _____[7] help them get into space. To reach space, the

_____[8] need to make the spacecraft attain a speed of _____[9]

kilometers per second. This speed is called the "orbital _____"[10] and

happens 190 kilometers above the Earth's surface. The _____[11] can now

freely orbit the Earth. However, if the _____[12] is headed for further

destinations, such as the Moon, _____[13] speed needs to increase to twelve

kilometers per second. _____[14] speed is called "escape velocity" and

means the spacecraft _____[15] broken away from the Earth's pull, or

gravity.

To _____[16] further again, for example to another

planet such as _____[17], the spacecraft must be

launched from Earth at a _____[18] (speed and

direction) greater than the "escape velocity." The craft

_____[19] then go into "solar orbit" to carry it to

_____[20] target planet. The Viking space probe has

sent back _____[21] information from orbiting and landing on Mars.

Spacecraft

1. What is special about the factories that build spacecraft?

_____

_____

_____

2. What is the biggest problem faced by any spacecraft?

_____

_____

_____

3. What makes it difficult for a spacecraft to enter into space?

_____

_____

4. When is "orbital velocity" reached?

_____

_____

5. What is the difference between "orbital velocity" and "escape velocity"?

_____

_____

_____

6. Give meanings for these terms.

(a) velocity _____

_____

(b) gravity _____

_____

7. If a spacecraft can travel eight kilometers per second using "orbital velocity," how far will it travel in…

1 minute? _____

10 minutes? _____

30 minutes? _____

8. Where would you like future rockets to travel? Give reasons for your answer.

_____

People in Space

The first spacecraft was launched by the Soviet Union on October 4, 1957. It was called Sputnik 1. This event began the space age. The first human in space was Soviet cosmonaut Yuri Gagarin. The flight in which he orbited the Earth was made on April 12, 1961 aboard his spacecraft Vostok 1. On February 20, 1962, John Glenn became the first American to orbit the Earth. Since these early times, many thousands of spacecraft have been launched. Scientists' next target was the Moon. Apollo 8 astronauts orbited the Moon ten times in December 1968. Then, on July 20, 1969, Neil Armstrong and Edwin "Buzz" Aldrin became the first humans to step onto the Moon. Further explorations saw the launch of the first space shuttle in April 1981. This was the first manned spacecraft designed to be reused.

When people go into space they must be protected because space has no air and the temperatures can be very hot and very cold. Spacecraft and space suits must provide people with this protection. They must also allow people to breathe, eat, drink, sleep and keep clean. Food and drink on a spacecraft must be easy to prepare and healthy. To keep clean, astronauts bathe with wet towels. When they sleep, they use special sleeping bags which strap them to a soft surface and their pillow. This stops them floating and bouncing around the cabin while they are asleep.

Astronauts' space suits provide a life support system for when they venture outside the spacecraft.

Write key notes about people in space. Use these questions to help your note taking.

1. Who was the first person in space?

2. What must people be protected from in space?

3. How do people sleep in space?

- _____
- _____
- _____
- _____
- _____
- _____

People in Space

The first spacecraft was launched by the Soviet Union _____[1] October 4, 1957. It was called Sputnik 1. This _____[2] began the space age. The first human in space _____[3] Soviet cosmonaut Yuri Gagarin. The flight in which he _____[4] the Earth was made on the April 12, 1961 _____[5] his spacecraft Vostok 1. On February 20, 1962, John _____[6] became the first American to orbit the Earth. Since _____[7] early times, many thousands of spacecraft have been launched. _____[8] next target was the Moon. Apollo 8 astronauts orbited _____[9] Moon ten times in December 1968. Then, on July _____[10] , 1969, Neil Armstrong and Edwin "Buzz" Aldrin became the first _____[11] to step onto the Moon. Further explorations saw the _____[12] of the first space shuttle in April 1981. This _____[13] the first manned spacecraft designed to be reused.

When _____[14] go into space they must be protected because space _____[15] no air and the temperatures can be very hot _____[16] very cold. Spacecraft and space suits must provide people _____[17] this protection. They must also allow people to breathe, _____[18], drink, sleep and keep clean. Food and drink on _____[19] spacecraft must be easy to prepare and healthy. To _____[20] clean, astronauts bathe with wet towels. When they sleep, _____[21] use special sleeping bags which strap them to a _____[22] surface and their pillow. This stops them floating and _____[23] around the cabin while they are asleep.

Astronauts' space _____[24] provide a life support system for when they venture _____[25] the spacecraft.

People in Space

1. What must a spacecraft and space suit allow people to do?

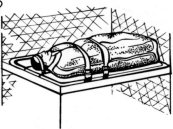

_____

_____

_____

2. How do astronauts keep themselves clean?

_____

_____

_____

3. Why do astronauts need special sleeping bags?

_____

_____

_____

4. Why do you think food and drinks in a spacecraft must be easy to prepare and healthy?

_____

_____

5. Imagine your favorite food. How do you think you would need to change it or package it to make it easy to eat in space?

_____

_____

_____

_____

Draw your product.

6. Complete the timeline below with important "space travel" dates and events.

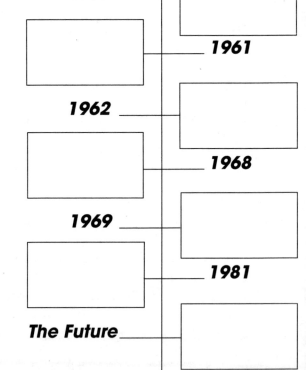

1957

1961

1962

1968

1969

1981

The Future

The Future in Space

Scientists are planning to put a base on the Moon soon after the year 2000. A lot of people believe a Moon base is an important step towards exploring the rest of the Solar System, and perhaps creating a base on Mars. Scientists also believe that the Moon could provide such things as oxygen or metals.

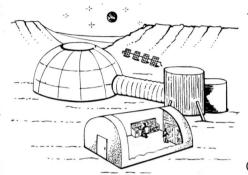

The next great step forward will be sending people to Mars. If such a trip happens, it will take the astronauts a year to get to Mars and a year to return. The spacecraft that would carry these astronauts would have to be large enough to carry all the fuel, food, water and other supplies, plus give the astronauts a comfortable place to live, for the entire journey.

Once near Mars, the spacecraft would need to orbit the planet. Perhaps a smaller craft could then be sent down to the surface of the planet. People could walk on the planet and gather samples of the soil and rocks and later take off to join the main ship for the return trip to Earth.

With space stretching so far into endless unknowns, the future for space travel and discoveries is limited only by our scientific technology. Who knows what lies ahead for future generations; perhaps living in space and traveling freely between planets and galaxies is closer than we think.

Write key notes below about future in space. Use these questions to help you with your note taking.

1. When will the Moon base be built?   2. What is the next step in space travel?

3. How long does a journey to Mars take?

- _____
- _____
- _____
- _____
- _____
- _____
- _____
- _____

The Future in Space

Scientists are planning to put a base on the _____[1] soon after the year

2000. A lot of people _____[2] a Moon base is an important step towards

exploring _____[3] rest of the Solar System, and perhaps creating a

_____[4] on Mars. Scientists also believe that the Moon could

_____[5] such things as oxygen or metals.

The next great _____[6] forward will be sending people to Mars. If such

_____[7] trip happens, it will take the astronauts a

year _____[8] get to Mars and a year to return. The

_____[9] that would carry these astronauts would

have to be _____[10] enough to carry all the fuel,

food, water and _____[11] supplies, plus give

the astronauts a comfortable place to

_____[12], for the entire journey. Once near Mars, the spacecraft

_____[13] need to orbit the planet. Perhaps a smaller craft

_____[14] then be sent down to the surface of the _____[15].

People could walk on the planet and gather samples _____[16] the soil and

rocks and later take off to _____[17] the main ship for the return trip to Earth.

_____[18] space stretching so far into endless unknowns, the future

_____[19] space travel and discoveries is limited only by our

_____[20] technology. Who knows what lies ahead for future generations;

_____[21] living in space and traveling freely between planets and

_____[22] is closer than we think.

The Future in Space

1. When are scientists planning a Moon base?

_____

_____

_____

2. Why is this an important step in space travel?

_____

_____

_____

3. Where do scientists aim to go after the Moon? _____

_____

4. Why do you think they have chosen this planet? _____

_____

_____

5. How long does it take to get to Mars and back to Earth?

four years   six years   three years   two years

6. Why would a spacecraft to Mars need to be large? _____

_____

_____

7. Do you think there could be other life in space? Give reasons for your answer.

_____

_____

_____

_____

Living in Space

Astronauts eat, sleep, work, wash and have fun in space, just like we do on Earth. There are some things they just can't do, like go shopping or to the park, rent videos or have takeout for dinner.

As there is no gravity, astronauts have to be careful when eating their food because it can easily float away. Astronauts tend to eat sticky foods, as foods that crumble easily are not suitable for eating in space. Food is generally dehydrated for space consumption, so it weighs less and takes up less space in the spacecraft. Water is added and mixed with the food before eating so it isn't too dry. Astronauts can have hot drinks or use hot water to make the food hot, but there is no refrigerator on the spacecraft, so they can't have any cold drinks. All trash needs to be collected and brought back to Earth with the spacecraft, as there aren't any trash cans in space. Going to the toilet is pretty easy, the toilet in the spacecraft uses air flow to carry waste away from the astronaut's body into space.

The lack of gravity also causes some difficulty when it is time for the astronauts to sleep. Some astronauts float gently around the cabin of the spacecraft, occasionally bouncing off walls while they sleep. Others prefer to zip themselves securely into a special sleeping bag, which keeps them in one place while they sleep. They can even strap a pillow to their head while they sleep if they want to.

The space shuttle does not have a bath or shower on board, so keeping clean is quite an adventure. Astronauts carefully take a sponge bath to keep their bodies clean. They brush their teeth in the usual way, but must be careful that blobs of toothpaste don't float away into the cabin.

Even though life in space is similar to that on Earth, astronauts have to do things differently from how we do them on Earth.

Write key notes about living in space. Use these questions to help your note taking.

1. What do astronauts do in space?
2. How are things different in space?
3. How do astronauts keep clean in space?

- _____
- _____
- _____
- _____
- _____

Living in Space

Astronauts eat, sleep, work, wash and have fun in _____[1], just like we

do on Earth. There are some _____[2] they just can't do, like go

shopping or to_____[3] park, rent videos or have takeout for dinner.

As _____[4] is no gravity, astronauts have to be careful when _____[5]

their food because it can easily float away. Astronauts _____[6] to eat sticky foods,

as foods that crumble easily _____[7] not suitable for eating in space. Food is

generally _____[8] for space consumption, so it weighs less and takes

_____[9] less space in the spacecraft. Water is added and _____[10]

with the food before eating so it isn't too _____[11]. Astronauts can have hot drinks

or use hot water _____[12] make the food hot, but there is no refrigerator

_____[13] the spacecraft, so they can't have any cold drinks. _____[14]

trash needs to be collected and brought back to _____[15] with the spacecraft,

as there aren't any trash cans _____[16] space. Going to the

toilet is pretty easy, the _____[17] in the spacecraft uses air flow

to carry waste _____[18] from the astronaut's body into space.

The lack of _____[19] also causes some difficulty when it is time for

_____[20] astronauts to sleep. Some astronauts float gently around the

_____[21] of the spacecraft, occasionally bouncing off walls while they

_____[22]. Others prefer to zip themselves securely into a special _____[23]

bag, which keeps them in one place while they _____[24]. They can even strap a

pillow to their head _____[25] they sleep if they want to.

The space shuttle _____[26] not have a bath or shower on board, so

_____[27] clean is quite an adventure. Astronauts carefully take a

_____[28] bath to keep their bodies clean. They brush their _____[29]

in the usual way, but must be careful that _____[30] of toothpaste don't float

away into the cabin.

Even _____[31] life in space is similar to that on Earth, _____[32]

have to do things differently from how we do _____[33] on Earth.

Living in Space

1. List three things astronauts can do in space.

   (a) _____

   (b) _____

   (c) _____

2. List three things astonauts cannot do in space.

   (a) _____

   (b) _____

   (c) _____

3. How does gravity help us on Earth? _____

   _____

4. Do you think food would taste differently in space? _____

   Explain. _____

   _____

5. Do you think it would be easy to fall asleep in space? _____

   Explain. _____

6. Why is it important to keep all trash and bring it back to Earth?

   _____

   _____

7. Design a sleeping bag that could be used in space. Include labels and any special features.

Answers

The Milky Way

Page 7

1. of 2. groups 3. Milky 4. the 5. stars
6. bulge 7. arms 8. The 9. Solar 10. those 11. its
12. orbit 13. galaxy 14. galaxy 15. bulge
16. known 17. of 18. are 19. everything
20. distances 21. year 22. galaxy 23. 300,000

Page 8

1. (L) Galaxies are large groups of stars, dust, gases and planets clustered together.
2. (L) The Milky Way is a spiral galaxy.
3. (I) Teacher check
4. (I) They both orbit around a central body.
5. (L) A light year is the distance light travels in one year.
6. (E) It would take 100,000 years.
7. (L) (a) A black hole.
   (b) Its gravitational pull is so great that everything, even light, gets sucked into the hole.
8. (L) A sphere of stars surrounding the disk and bulge of our Milky Way Galaxy.
9. Teacher check

The Solar System

Page 10

1. is 2. Solar 3. a 4. travel 5. moons 6. center
7. times 8. put 9. the 10. over 11. planets
12. Sun 13. and 14. the 15. rock 16. a
17. Jupiter 18. left-over 19. of 20. are 21. tail
22. or

Page 11

1. (L) Our Solar System consists of the Sun, planets, moons, meteoroids, asteroids, comets and dust.
2. (L) The Milky Way.
3. (I) Answers may vary
4. (I) Asteroids are small metal or rock objects found mostly in a belt orbiting the Sun between Mars and Jupiter.
5. (L) (c)
6. (I) Teacher check
7. (L) (a) Pluto (b) Mercury (c) comet (d) asteroid (e) planetoid
8. (E) Answers may vary
9. Teacher check

The Sun

Page 13

1. our 2. glowing 3. All 4. appears 5. the
6. million 7. eight 8. nearest 9. a 10. than
11. made 12. the 13. million 14. in 15. it
16. to 17. essential 18. Without 19. Plants
20. a 21. the 22. out 23. light 24. of

Page 14

1. (a) True (b) True (c) False (d) False
2. (L) Sirius
3. (I) A stars over 1,000 times larger than our Sun
4. (I) Answers may vary
5. (I) Teacher check
6. (L) Earth, heat, light
7. (I) hot gases, Star, "yellow dwarf," essential to life on Earth, center of Solar System
8. (E) Teacher check

Mercury

Page 16

1. is 2. to 3. it 4. a 5. orbit 6. Romans 7. gods
8. It 9. once 10. the 11. a 12. Earth 13. that
14. and 15. formed 16. very 17. on 18. hot
19. of 20. be 21. side 22. can 23. None
24. survive 25. lack

Page 17

1. (L) closest, to half the size
2. (L) Mercury is hard to see even with a telescope because it is small and close to the bright glare of the Sun.
3. (L) Eighty-eight days.
4. (L) Ancient Romans; "swift messenger" of their gods.
5. (I) Answers may vary
6. (L) Meteorites or comets hitting its surface.
7. (I) intense temperatures, lack of oxygen
8. (E) Teacher check

The Moon

Page 19

1. Although 2. sky 3. moonlight 4. If 5. the
6. the 7. gravity 8. 60 kg 9. Even 10. each
11. other 12. with 13. no 14. is 15. formed
16. surface 17. plains 18. is 19. space 20. be
21. first 22. one 23. landed 24. expeditions
25. more

Page 20

1. (L) "Moonlight" is the reflection of the Sun off the Moon's surface. The Moon doesn't give off its own light.
2. (I) They would weigh 20 kg.
3. (E) Answers may vary
4. (I) Neil Armstrong became the first human to step on the Moon. He was part of the crew of the Apollo 11 spacecraft, which landed July 20, 1969.
5. (E) Answers may vary
6. (I) Earth - blue, watery, cloud-covered planet; living things: atmosphere; stronger gravity than Moon; larger than Moon
   Moon - smaller than Earth; cratered surface; no air, wind, water, clouds or living things; temperatures can vary from – 240°C to 130°C.

Answers

7. (a) barren - infertile, no living things
   (b) gravity - the force that causes everything to fall towards the center of the Earth
8. Teacher check

Comets

Page 22

1. System 2. a 3. surrounds 4. nucleus 5. head 6. ball 7. kilometers 8. and 9. dioxide 10. close 11. and 12. and 13. Sun 14. streak 15. of 16. ice 17. turn 18. Earth 19. and 20. seen 21. close 22. telescope 23. comets 24. Comet 25. predicted 26. that 27. years 28. beyond 29. in

Page 23

1. (L) In our Solar System orbiting the Sun.
2. (L) Comets are made from frozen gases, ice and rocky dust particles.
3. (I) (a) nucleus - center of a comet with a hard, icy core
   (b) tail - solar winds blow gases and dust away from the head of the comet to leave a trail
   (c) coma - a cloudy atmosphere surrounding the nucleus
4. (L) As a comet approaches the Sun, it loses some of its ice and dust. Eventually a comet will lose all its ice and dust.
5. (L) "meteor" or "shooting star"
6. (I) Teacher check
7. (E) Teacher check
8. Teacher check
9. comet, telescope, ice, dust, rock, meteors, coma, size, Earth, Sun, pieces

Meteors

Page 25

1. seen 2. shooting 3. when 4. enters 5. Air 6. hot 7. lasts 8. actually 9. they 10. of 11. ever 12. and 13. at 14. types 15. rock 16. of 17. may 18. weigh 19. substantial 20. small 21. surface 22. the 23. thought 24. that 25. meteorites 26. preserved

Page 26

1. (L) Meteors are bright streaks of light that can be seen at night as they enter the Earth's atmosphere.
2. (L) Air friction heats the meteor causing it to glow.
3. (I) (a) meteoroid - a piece of metal or rock in space
   (b) meteorite - a meteoroid that reaches the Earth's surface
4. (I) If it's too small it burns up in the Earth's atmosphere and if too big it may explode before reaching the ground.
5. (E) Answers may vary

6. (L) rock minerals or iron particles
7. (a) True (b) False (c) True (d) True (e) False
8. Teacher check

Asteroids

Page 28

1. the 2. Sometimes 3. be 4. up 5. together 6. in 7. Thousands 8. Ceres 9. to 10. in 11. Most 12. six 13. while 14. combined 15. Moon 16. the 17. may 18. Hermes 19. a 20. This 21. major 22. extinction

Page 29

1. (L) Most asteroids can be found in the asteroid belt which is between Mars and Jupiter.
2. (L) Thought to be small, rocky remains of a planet which broke up millions of years ago or particles that never came together when planets were formed.
3. (L) Ceres: discovered 1801, measures 1,000 km in diameter.
4. (I) A large asteroid hit the Earth sixty-five million years ago causing weather and climate changes which could have led to the extinction of the dinosaurs.
5. (E) Answers may vary
6. (a) planetoid - asteroid
   (b) crash - collision
   (c) death of a species - extinction
7. (E) Teacher check
8. Mars, minerals, carbon, belt, extinct, collided, Earth, Jupiter, Ceres, asteroid, years, weather, planet, climate

Space

Page 31

1. to 2. from 3. are 4. Earth 5. that 6. you 7. out 8. is 9. is 10. thousands 11. space 12. space 13. this 14. measured 15. the 16. space 17. in 18. the 19. to 20. light 21. space 22. a

Page 32

1. (L) Space is the empty areas in which all stars and other objects in the universe move.
2. (L) the Earth's atmosphere
3. (L) 95 kilometers from the Earth's surface.
4. (I) "interplanetary space" - distance between planets; Sun controls orbits and planet movements, distances measured in millions of kilometers "interstellar space" - distances between stars; measured in light years; distance light travels in one year; nearest star Proxima Centauri - 4.5 light years away "intergalactic space" - space between galaxies; huge unimaginable distances to measure

Answers

5. (L) The space just above the air contains dust, meteoroids and spacecraft.
6. (I) Nine years
7. (E) Teacher check

Spacecraft

Page 34

1. These 2. bit 3. All 4. being 5. is 6. very 7. to 8. rockets 9. eight 10. velocity 11. spacecraft 12. spacecraft 13. its 14. This 15. has 16. travel 17. Mars 18. velocity 19. would 20. the 21. valuable

Page 35

1. (L) Factories that build spacecraft must be very clean.
2. (L) The biggest problem found by any spacecraft is getting into space.
3. (I) The pull of the Earth's gravity makes it hard for a spacecraft to enter space.
4. (L) "Orbital velocity" is reached at a speed of 8 km per second.
5. (I) The difference is in speed - 4 km per second.
6. (a) speed, rate of motion
    (b) the force that causes everything to fall towards the center of the Earth
7. 480 kms, 4,800 kms, 14,400 kms.
8. (E) Teacher check

People in Space

Page 37

1. on 2. event 3. was 4. orbited 5. aboard 6. Glenn 7. these 8. Scientists' 9. the 10. 20 11. humans 12. launch 13. was 14. people 15. has 16. and 17. with 18. eat 19. a 20. keep 21. they 22. soft 23. bouncing 24. suits 25. outside

Page 38

1. (L) They must allow people to breathe, eat, drink, sleep and keep clean.
2. (L) They bathe themselves with wet towels.
3. (L) They use special sleeping bags to strap them down. This stops them floating and bouncing around the cabin when they're asleep.
4. (E) Answers may vary
5. (E) Teacher check
6. (I) 1957 - first spacecraft launched by Soviets
    1961 - first person in space, cosmonaut Yuri Gagarin
    1962 - John Glenn, first to orbit Earth
    1968 - Apollo 8 orbit Moon ten times
    1969 - first humans on Moon; Neil Armstrong and Edwin "Buzz" Aldrin, crew of Apollo 11
    1981- first space shuttle launched
    Future - Answers may vary

The Future in Space

Page 40

1. Moon 2. believe 3. the 4. base 5. provide 6. step 7. a 8. to 9. spacecraft 10. large 11. other 12. live 13. would 14. could 15. planet 16. of 17. join 18. With 19. for 20. scientific 21. perhaps 22. galaxies

Page 41

1. (L) Scientists are planning a Moon base soon after the year 2000.
2. (L) It is the first step towards exploring the rest of our Solar System and perhaps a base on Mars.
3. (L) Sending people to Mars
4. (E) Answers may vary
5. (I) two years
6. (I) Spacecraft would need to carry enough fuel, food, water and other supplies plus also give astronauts a comfortable place to live for up to two years of traveling.
7. (E) Answers may vary

Living in Space

Page 43

1. space 2. things 3. the 4. there 5. eating 6. tend 7. are 8. dehydrated 9. up 10. mixed 11. dry 12. to 13. on 14. All 15. Earth 16. in 17. toilet 18. away 19. gravity 20. the 21. cabin 22. sleep 23. sleeping 24. sleep 25. while 26. does 27. keeping 28. sponge 29. teeth 30. blobs 31. though 32. astronauts 33. them

Page 44

1. (L) eat, sleep, work, wash, have fun
2. (L) go shopping, go to the park, rent videos, have takeout for dinner
3. (I) Gravity is a force which draws us to Earth like a magnet. It stops us from floating into space.
4. (E) Answers may vary.
5. (E) Answers may vary.
6. (I) So as not to pollute space.
7. (E) Teacher check.

Abstract nouns are the names we give to the things we can't physically touch such as "fear" and "idea." We can experience fear and have an idea but we can't actually touch them or hold them in our hands. Complete the crossword puzzle of abstract nouns below. The first letter of each noun is given. A dictionary may be helpful!

Across

1. disgrace
2. security
4. knowledge
6. jealousy
8. enthusiasm
9. unhappiness
12. trustworthiness
15. avarice
16. sorrow
19. fear
20. viciousness
21. truthfulness

Down

1. astonishment
2. coyness
3. longing
5. kindness
7. conceit
10. self-esteem
11. peace
13. hostility
14. liberty
17. renown
18. veracity

Challenge!

1. **Write three abstract nouns of your own.**

   (a) _____

   (b) _____

   (c) _____